DEBATING FAKE NEWS

A Guide with Critical Thinking Strategies on How to Extract the Truth from Fake News and Alternative Facts in the Media

Copyright © 2017 Reina Donovan
All rights reserved.
ISBN: 978-1974582853

© Copyright 2017 by Reina Donovan- All rights reserved.

The following eBook is reproduced below with the goal of providing information that is as accurate and as reliable as possible. Regardless, purchasing this eBook can be seen as consent to the fact that both the publisher and the author of this book are in no way experts on the topics discussed within, and that any recommendations or suggestions made herein are for entertainment purposes only. Professionals should be consulted as needed before undertaking any of the action endorsed herein.

This declaration is deemed fair and valid by both the American Bar Association and the Committee of Publishers Association and is legally binding throughout the United States.

Furthermore, the transmission, duplication or reproduction of any of the following work, including precise information, will be considered an illegal act, irrespective whether it is done electronically or in print. The legality extends to creating a secondary or tertiary copy of the work or a recorded copy and is only allowed with express written consent of the Publisher. All additional rights are reserved.

The information in the following pages is broadly considered to be a truthful and accurate account of facts, and as such any inattention, use or misuse of the information in question by the reader will render any resulting actions solely under their purview. There are no scenarios in which the publisher or the original author of this work can be in any fashion deemed liable for any hardship or damages that may befall them after undertaking information described herein.

Additionally, the information found on the following pages is intended for informational purposes only and should thus be considered, universal. As befitting its nature, the information presented is without assurance regarding its continued validity or interim quality. Trademarks that mentioned are done without written consent and can in no way be considered an endorsement from the trademark holder.

Table of Contents

INTRODUCTION 7

CHAPTER 1: *What is Propaganda?* 11

CHAPTER 2: *The History of Propaganda* 23

CHAPTER 3: *Modern Forms of Propaganda* 38

CHAPTER 4: *Are Modern News Outlets Legitimate Sources?* 53

CHAPTER 5: *Who Owns these Media Platforms?* 77

CHAPTER 6: *What is Fake News and How can you Spot it?* 105

CHAPTER 7 *Tips for Evaluating Information Online* 121

CONCLUSION 133

INTRODUCTION

Congratulations on downloading your personal copy of *Debating Fake News: A Guide with Critical Thinking Strategies on How to Extract the Truth from Fake News and Alternative Facts in the Media.* Thank you for doing so.

There aren't many people who have confidence in the stories and information they hear from professional news outlets or family and friends. However, large majorities of people have at least a bit of trust in these sources. Social media, on the other hand, gets far lower scores on trust. Given the fact that a lot of people get their news from these sources, this is an issue. Let's look at some related facts on this phenomenon.

- **Local and International News:** Only 22 percent of Americans trust online or offline news organizations and less than 20 percent have the same opinion about national news organizations. Although the amount of people who say they have trust in these groups is very low, there are still some who believe them.

- **Social Media:** Social media sources, however, are trusted by hardly any, at only 4 percent of people saying they believe the information found on their news feeds. And only 7 percent of people believe the news they read on websites such as Facebook or Twitter.

- **Democrats and Republicans:** Democrats are likelier to have trust in news outlet information. 27 percent of democrats trust what they hear from these sources, compared to just 15 percent of those on the right. Most adults in America believe that these news outlets are extremely biased.

- **Keeping Politics in Check:** About 75 percent of American citizens believe that these news outlets are there to keep political leaders from doing what they shouldn't do, but this same amount of Americans thinks that the outlets show favor to one side or the other. And those on the more conservative side of things are likelier to believe that the news outlets are biased.

As you can see, it's getting harder and harder for Americans to believe what they hear from the news, even when it's from a source that they trusted previously. This book will help you understand why it's so hard to determine the truth and how you can learn to separate the facts from the fiction. Did you know that media consolidation is making fake news more and more common as the truth gets swept under the rug? This, in combination with intellectual laziness, will have a harmful impact on our society over time, if we don't do something about it.

In this book, we will go over the history of propaganda, how it's still being used today, and what you can do protect yourself from it. We will also cover how you can determine what is true and which sources are reliable when you are seeking information. There are plenty of books on this subject on the market, thanks again for choosing this one! Every effort was made to ensure it is full of as much useful information as possible. Please enjoy!

CHAPTER 1
What is Propaganda?

"Fake news" has become somewhat of a buzz word, but when is the first time you heard it? For most, it was first heard around the time of the last presidential election. Many people consume plenty of business and political news, and for them that was still the first time they had heard that term in the mainstream outlets. Right after the presidential election ended, it seemed like the top leaders in each party had something new to focus on and accuse each other of; fake news.

The intention here appeared to start with a story about the way the "news" or "media" needed to be held to higher standards of truth. This, to some, should be quite worrying. Some people within the political sphere started using that term to describe mainstream news. Soon after this new term came about, people on Facebook started pivoting toward the conversation of the mainstream media and fake news.

AP, NYT, CNN, all of those organizations, were now (and are now) considered fake news to some people. Nowadays, it appears like almost nothing is truly bipartisan. Instead, everything is more polarized than ever. During this time, everything appears to be some kind of deception.

The Polarized Extremes:

Certain media outlets don't try hard to hide their political leanings, ethos, and methodology, but others don't make it as obvious. Either way, there's still intention in the background of what they are presenting. Do you know anyone who watches the news at 6 PM anymore? People don't as much anymore because these news outlets seem to be leaning further and further toward opposite ends of the sphere.

For years now, the division between political and editorial opinion has been diminishing. Now, it's all about saying the most shocking thing possible and drawing people to click bait websites. Even televised news appears to be getting more and more "click-bait like."

What is Click Bait doing to Journalism?

The news, nowadays, appears to be trying to produce moral panic. Click bait (and click bait-inspired news stories) hardly ever have content that is worth reporting on, but it attracts curiosity and viewers. The believe appears to be that people will keep listening for the "real" content as soon as they are pulled in by nonsense. This isn't entirely a bad thing. A lot of businesses and news outlets have been modernized and transformed by the Internet and digital options. Customers have benefited greatly from the simplicity and cost-effectiveness of digitized businesses, but there are some downsides.

As media outlets compete for viewers, renewed pressure must be put on legacy media, as well. Broadcasters have to try to pull their viewers in using click bait. Click bait is defined as something eye catching that makes readers want to click.

It usually creates income based on how many clicks it gets and its costs are covered by advertisers. For instance, the CBC (Canada's public broadcaster) uses a lot of click bait, even though the journalists don't necessarily agree with it and the public doesn't either. One of journalism's best qualities is skepticism, but the Internet has replaced this with enthusiasm.

Debating Fake News:

No change, in terms of technology can be completely reversed. Sometimes, it may be paused, slowed, or questioned. Many people blame this new advent of "fake news" and increasing polarity on the medium that is being used with it; technology. If journalism will become reliable, honest, and trustworthy again, it must resist the bad qualities of digitalism in order to give the public what they need; real news and truth.

Needing the Truth:

The digital format of the news nowadays is just that, a digital format. The technology will only survive and thrive if there's something valuable to share. The public now feels starved of information and wants to know what to do. This book is a good place to start, as it will give you tools on how to decipher the truth from the fake.

The Importance of Quality Information:

Without the desire to understand the other side of your beliefs, and without good sources to explore them, it's too easy to get locked into your own opinions. Even though it may make you angry to withstand too much of the other side, especially with the style news is presented in these days, it's beneficial to learn how to articulate and define your reasons for opposition, instead of just agreeing.

<u>Looking for Motives:</u>

The best place to begin is to start questioning and looking for the motives behind the news you are hearing or reading and understanding which narrative they are pushing. This will help you both articulate your position and think for yourself. Even outlets that are considered "alternative news" should be approached with caution, such as Vice and WikiLeaks. Even if a source is considered a propaganda machine, does this mean it should be ignored? Here are some questions you should be asking yourself anytime you consume news online or otherwise.

- Who owns this news outlet?

- What is the motive behind this?

- What narrative is being sold here?

- What proof is there to support this?

Asking yourself all of these questions is a great way to go about protecting yourself from misinformation. It also helps to foster an environment that thrives on discussion instead of fights and ad hominem.

What is Propaganda?

In order to understand how fake news came to be, it's crucial to first understand propaganda. Propaganda is not easily defined, but most people can agree that propaganda involves beliefs or ideas that are propagated on purpose. Propaganda uses word substitutes and words to reach a certain goal, including songs, parades, exhibits, graphs, drawings, pictures, and more. Propaganda is, of course, used in very controversial ways, but it can also promote things are aren't controversial and are generally accepted or acceptable.

Therefore, different types of it exist. Propaganda can be subversive, deceitful, and selfish, or it can be honest and working toward good things. Propaganda may be either open or hidden, logic-based or based on emotion, or a mixture of logic and emotion.

A Historical Example of Propaganda:

In 1940, in the Spring time, armies were facing columns in Germany, but not much action was happening near the front, and some soldiers from France had the time to listen in on a broadcast being given by their enemy. The radio voice asked where the English were, but the broadcaster was speaking French as the soldiers listened with uneasy ears. The voice then said that the English comrades are filling the night clubs in Paris, hanging out behind the lines and sleeping with the French soldiers' wives.

Radio Propaganda in Britain:

This was propaganda given by the German to sow suspicion in the Frenchmen's minds, create division, and cause doubt about the Frenchmen's allies. A couple months later, some Londoners were drinking beer at their local pub. The Frenchmen have already signed the terms of Hitler's armistice, but Britain has not. The man keeping the pub turned the tavern radio to a broadcaster in Berlin.

The voice on the radio said that England was ready to be invaded and completely doomed. It said that England was asking for peace instead of destruction, and that Germany would provide it. This is a perfect example of fear-based propaganda.

Radio Propaganda in the USA:

That next year (1941), the USA was still neutral, even though the Navy was being strengthened and the Army in America was training. One American is listening to the radio at home and hears a broadcast being sent to the USA from Germany. It said that the Germans had only positive and friendly feelings toward the USA, where many German descendants were living. The voice was intentionally sweetened as it said that a victory for Germany in the war would not threaten either British or American democracy.

This was the voice of propaganda and appeasement, a strategy trying to hypnotize Americans with the idea of the Nazi's peaceful intentions in their war. It was only months later that Germany declared war against the ones they said they had only positive feelings towards.

CHAPTER 2
The History of Propaganda

Whether a propagandist is working in a war-related or peace-related situation, he will use specific tools to affect and control attitudes and opinions. Which tools are these? One of them is stimulation and the other one is suggestion.

Stimulation and Suggestion in Propaganda:

Someone trying to force propaganda will attempt to stimulate people to accept his assertions without doubt or challenge, or acts the way he wishes for them to act. The concept of using stimulation or suggestion for propaganda is there to lead people to accept something without any good logical reasons for doing so. A propagandist will typically attempt to avoid critical questions or reactions from those listening and that is why suggestion is so important as a tool for propaganda.

How do propagandists use that tactic? They do it by making positive and broad statements. When the propagandist presents his ideas in familiar, simple words and refuses to suggest or admit that another side exists to his position, this is propaganda. Hitler's direct and brutal suggestion that the Jews stabbed the Germans in the back during World War II is a perfect example of this. Another instance of propaganda from this time period is the Nazi assertion that President Roosevelt and Prime Minister Churchill were warmongers.

Commercial Advertising and Suggestion:

Suggestion is a tactic used widely in commercial types of advertisement. One obvious instance of this is that a certain company's brand of vitamins will give you energy and get rid of your exhaustion.

- **Indirect Statements:** There is another, subtler form of propaganda, which is the use of indirect statements, insinuations, or hints in speech. One only has to look at the world of advertising to see this method at work. A commercial company sponsoring an orchestra to create a good feeling for the listener in regards to a product is one such example. At times, programs are built to portray the culture and life of a different nation, which is another use of propaganda.

- **Using Desires:** Yet another propaganda method is appealing to desires of the listener. Psychologists claim that desire has a lot to do with personal beliefs. So some people could support a economic scheme that is doomed to fail, just because they want to have income when they get older. Other people will believe in some type of psychological scheme just to try to make their personality better.

Propagandists Studying Opinion:

A propagandist who is self-interested will pay attention to the opinions of the public to discover what individuals are against or for, to figure out which labels he should use to create the reactions he desires.

The Power of Language:

The propagandist knows that "law and order," "Americanism," and "justice" are all words that people will respond favorably to. He knows that it will create favorable reactions and therefore uses these terms. He might also use terms that others will reject in order to further his own interests, like "un-American" or "radical." Hitler was adept at appealing to many different German groups of people. His appeals had little to no consistency, but he has suggested plenty of panaceas (or cure all answers) for unhappy or discontented groups.

Appealing to Human Desires:

The man who is concerned with advertising tries to appeal to both the insecurities and the desires of his customer. The wish to be healthy and strong, to be accepted by others socially, to be handsome, are all used to sell something to the customer. There is always a perfume, soap, or drug product designed to help him attain his desire. Any person who is used to seeing ads will be able to remember countless examples of advertising agencies attempting to promote these products.

Getting Ideas to Stick:

A propagandist who is skilled at what he does knows how to make ideas stick in people's minds. Due to this information, the propagandist uses symbolic forms, slogans, and key words to get people on his side. An ad slogan will pack a lot of meaning into a short phrase or sentence, with the intention of getting the sentiment noticed and remembered. These slogans get into your mind, not easily forgotten, and that is what they are designed for. When someone is selecting which product to purchase, it's only natural that the ad's slogan will pop up in his head.

Emotionalized Appeals:

Decades ago, advertisers figured out that appeals about the "reasons why" something was better than something else was not very effective on the human mind. For this reason, appeals were emotionalized and shortened, since most readers wouldn't be willing to sift through reasons why something was supposedly better than something else. If you look closely at commercials and even news stories, you will easily recognize this tactic happening in front of your eyes.

Propaganda in International Politics:

The history of propaganda in international politics is full of instances of slogans and buzz words. For instance, Hitler liked to use name-calling as a tactic and called democratic countries "Pluto-democracies." When he was trying to become more powerful, he claimed that the Versailles Treaty was a monstrous lie.

Slogans are not always Bad:

Although the propaganda of that nation and era both outside and inside of Germany was characterized by terror, most symbols and slogans are not like this. For instance, slogans from the Salvation Army or the Red Cross are designed to help support the community and war relief. At times, slogans have helped get people fired up for important and overall positive reasons. Propaganda definitely uses slogans, but also puts symbols to use. Symbols are solid representations of a thing, action, or idea. It's a sign that is meant to stand for another thing, like the propeller and wings for the U.S. Air Force.

Using Symbols in Propaganda:

A symbol in propaganda can be a statue, a picture, an image, a song, an object, or some other representation that conveys an idea to large numbers of people. It's a type of glue to hold together social groups of people. The skilled propagandist is well aware that symbols are an important part of the process and uses them to propagate both unfavorable and favorable attitudes and beliefs.

Symbols for Beliefs:

The usage of symbols can make likenesses for certain types of people. For instance, people have drawn symbols to stand for the college professor, taxpayer, and other types of people. Cartoonists have depicted the prohibitionist as a long-nosed, and tall figure, while a capitalist could be portrayed by a man in a dollar sign-covered suit. Within the last 50 years, Western nations have used popular symbols less and less, but a huge number of symbols have been made by communist, Nazi, and fascist states.

<u>Obvious Symbols in Nazism:</u>

The Nazis purposely made symbols that were so conspicuous and unmistakable that if citizens of the country didn't use them, they would be detected right away. Among these symbols were the swastika of course, uniforms, badges, and the Nazi salute. Even Hitler gave himself a special name, pretending that president was not official enough. The Nazi hierarchy, including Hitler used the word "non-Aryan" as a catch phrase and used it as a device to persecute minorities who weren't powerful or numerous enough to resist Nazi terrorists and their violence.

Slogans and catchwords abounded in the propaganda of the Nazis, created to impress Germans. The Nazi regime was fond of high-sounding, important phrases and words like "imperishable" and "immutable." Always opportunists, Nazis were quick to throw away slogans when they had already done what they were intended to do, then new ones were made and forced upon the German citizens.

Symbols in Japanese Propaganda:

The main symbol that was used to call the Japanese fighting men and civilians to action was the emperor. Higher-ups in Japan kept their internal power strong by making their emperor into a god, emphasizing and claiming his descent from the god of the sun. This was used to stimulate the enthusiasm of sailors and soldiers. The Japanese devised propaganda against the British and American, using "white exploiter" as their symbol of the enemy forces. They called imperialism "co-prosperity" as a way to try to win people over to sharing with similar races to the exclusion of others.

More about Co-Prosperity and the Japanese:

Another method that the propagandist uses is the element of prestige in human relationships. Psychologists do not all agree about how much the opinions and attitudes of people can be spurred by the idea of prestige alone, but it's apparent that the idea of prestige is important. For instance, parental influence over one's child, has to do with the prestige of that person's power knowledge, strength, and size.

Prestige and Expert Status in Propaganda:

Some groups or people resent opinions of experts and don't want to respond to the ideas of scientists and fact-finders. However, in politics, prestige does obviously matter. In political campaigns, the prestige of a successful businessperson is always a factor, particularly in prosperous times.

Prestige in Political Leadership and Military:

During wartime, people stress their military's prestige, and that of their political leadership. At times, that idea is built up using legends, yet another way to influence people's beliefs and attitudes. Typically, these legends are constructed from a small truth, but usually the resulting image is more similar to a fictional hero or character. The stories of Siegfried, Roland, and Ulysses, for instance, grew around strong and powerful warriors. Regardless of whether these legends are created on purpose or not, they are believed and accepted by people everywhere and therefore have an influence on how people act. Many people live within these symbols or legends.

<u>Powerful Mythmakers:</u>

Mussolini, Hitler, and those who followed them, were powerful makers of myth. Hitler was nearly deified by the Nazi regime and the methods used for mass hypnosis by the Germans at that time were tactics that are hard to understand as modern Americans. To the average American citizen, it's unthinkable that an uneducated, intense, fanatic man who was unschooled in politics and economics could be exalted into an infallible, powerful leader. He exacted obedience unquestioningly from his followers and was seen as someone who was never wrong.

How did so many German people accept this myth of Hitler's all-knowingness? Some believe that it's because the Germans wanted an end to the struggle that was going on. Others believe that Hitler was simply highly skilled in propaganda. Some even felt satisfied that they had a Great Father who would willingly take on responsibility for their wellbeing in exchange for their blind subordination and implicit faith. How does this relate to what we are experiencing today with the news and modern propaganda? Let's find out.

CHAPTER 3
Modern Forms of Propaganda

Freedom of speech and a free media are crucial in a democratic society and form the foundation of it. To put it another way, in the case that a nation's people don't have access to quality, unbiased, comprehensive, and accurate information, the democracy would no longer function and would fall apart. Although the media knows this well, ironically, illiteracy is becoming more and more common across the world and the ratio of nonsense to helpful information is declining.

This combination of factors has created a mix that makes it much easier for modern methods of propaganda to harm its readers and listeners into thinking that what they are reading is the one truth. Thankfully, people are starting to wise up to these techniques, meaning that the techniques are less likely to work on them.

Modern Methods of Propaganda:

If you start paying close attention, you will probably start to recognize these around you. Let's go over some of the popular propaganda methods used by mainstream media outlets:

- **Inducing Panic and Fear to Viewers:** Ensuring that those viewing or reading are fearful is a surefire way to make them bypass their logic and reason. Essentially, when someone is constantly panicked or afraid, they cannot think in a rational way and, therefore, will be a lot likelier to believe what they hear on the news or online. If anyone were to believe everything the media told them, they would feel paranoid just being at home.

- **Projecting Misdeeds or Faults:** If you want to discredit those who disagree with or criticize you, the easiest way to do this is to strike them under the belt and then claim that they are the ones who did that. This technique of propaganda is actually very common these days. Just envision the people who believe that climate change is the fault of humans not caring for our environment. More and more often, these people are called out on spreading lies since they don't have scientific data to prove their point of view.

- **Ad Hominem:** The trend happening at this moment, and even promoted by specific corporations in the media, is to disregard the opponents and critics as quickly as possible. Since dismissing ideas takes time, the quickest method for doing this is attacking that person's intelligence, sanity, morale, character, or credibility. In other words, they go straight for whatever is easiest to pick on and dismiss. Considering the fact that arguments like these often don't leave any real for real arguments or discussions, it's simply undemocratic.

- **Bullying Tactics:** If you're an opponent of an idea who is invited to have an argument or discussion on a particular subject, you will be eaten alive by the moderators unless you are extremely educated on the topic and confident in yourself. Guests get put into corners more often than they do not and the counterarguments of the one bullying win only because the guest is so ashamed, anxious, and uncomfortable that they have no choice but to relent.

- **Changing Facts in History:** A lot of people wonder how someone could try to lie about history, when the facts can easily be verified or disproven. But although this may be true for someone highly educated or informed, for someone operating under strict believes, it's much easier to just refuse to acknowledge certain facts than to make some effort to get the truth or possibly change his or her points of view. And when they one speaking is great at orating and is also considered an authority on the topic, even those who are educated or informed begin doubting what they know to be true. This can refer to both recent history and local issues in your area.

Don't be Scared of Propaganda:

Regardless of how you choose to define the word, don't be scared of propaganda. Not long ago, having a cautious approach was more important than being scared is now.

Attitudes toward Propaganda in History:

Propaganda was, at the time, basically the boogeyman. Writers and speakers saw it as something magical. Some told people at the time that everything we did was just because the propaganda was telling us to. For this reason, many people at the time believed that the creator of propaganda was hiding everywhere, ready to attack, and that everything that was told to us by him was for our own wellbeing. But both ideas here were false.

Not all Propaganda is Bad:

Some propaganda is actually a good thing and urges us to follow action that greatly benefits us. A lot of what people call propaganda is not trying to convince people of anything. In a country that is democratic, where we take freedom of expression for granted, no one should wish to get rid of all propaganda. Democracy is all about having rival points out in plan view. Decisions on questions, involving political matters too, need to be chosen by free individuals. This involves not closing our ears and eyes to opposing viewpoints, but looking at, evaluating them, and dismissing the ones that are not valid (after fair analysis).

<u>Propaganda and Fear:</u>

The ones who spread fear of the idea of propaganda are operating under the mistaken assumption that propaganda is enough to govern the opinion of the public. However, propaganda is only a single factor that has an influence on opinion. Sound knowledge based on facts, specific information, and data presented free from propaganda, all make up another crucial factor in how public opinion is formed. And many others exist, as well.

The trend of unreasonable panic toward propaganda is starting to level off, somewhat. People are beginning to realize that though some campaigns using these techniques have been successful, other similar ones have failed. This is evidence that propaganda, on its own, cannot shape the opinion of the public and that the process is more complex than this.

How can we Know what to Believe?

This is an idea that will be explored throughout the book. There is now propaganda out against propaganda, leading confused people to wonder how they can know what to believe. The best answer to this is that you can believe your own traditions and values, your own instincts, and your own common sense. In other words, believe in yourself before anything else. The principle of democracy calls for us to find out own answers on current issues or any others that pop up.

The Responsibility of Decision:

No one can get rid of the responsibility of making up their mind on questions that require answers. This is true with local politics, international policies, and even choosing one brand of laundry soap over another.

In making a decision on his own, the person may take a look at the propaganda that exists, while also considering that which exists outside of it, using each criterion and standard available to find the best answer.

Questions for Seeing through Propaganda:

One who is attempting to see through propaganda shouldn't forget that you can check the merits of information and check for any self-interests that lie behind it. Here are the questions you can employ in this situation:

- **Is this truly Propaganda?** Is a group or individual purposely trying to influence the action or opinion of those viewing this? And why?

- **Is this Information True?** The next question involves comparing independent sources to make sure the facts you're hearing or reading are real.

- **Which Parts Matter and which Don't?** The next question you can apply involves asking yourself which parts of the promotion matter and which don't.

- **Is the Action Selfish?** If some group or person is attempting to influence actions and opinions of others, is this for a selfish reason? Is this action going to benefit more than just that one person or group?

- **What is the End Result?** What does it seem as though the end result will be of what the propagandist individual or group is trying to push? Is it something positive?

Each of these questions can be summed up to simpler questions, such as where does this propaganda come from? What are the purposes behind this propaganda? Who benefits from this and what is it truly trying to say?

Propaganda and the News:

Although overvaluing propaganda can be a serious mistake, it's also a mistake to believe that everything on the radio and news is propaganda, or that propaganda is deceitful, improperly motivated, or self-seeking inherently. These specific outlets can be used in this way, of course, but they may also be utilized for positive purposes or material that has nothing to do with propaganda. We can start by checking out the example of the newspaper.

The Necessity of Freedom of Press:

Freedom of the American press is a must under the Constitution. This is because a democratic country is aware that freedom of opinion and expression, with the freedom of facts and without governmental restrictions, is needed for its citizens to be called to intelligent action.

Today's journalists have a responsibility to be disinterested, objective, and accurate with the facts they report. A newspaperman who has respect both for his work and himself must accept that responsibility. The well-trained, self-disciplined, and honest reporter should only be a propagandist for the truth and nothing else.

Disguised Propaganda:

Propaganda, does of course get involved with the press. At times, it can even be presented disguised as objective fact since the journalist wasn't smart enough or sufficiently trained to spot it for what it truly is.

At times, news outlets are even conscious pushers of propaganda, in headlines and news alike. And, at other times, propaganda is both news, and important to the readers, which results in the paper presenting the information and knowing the readers will evaluate it on their own.

The Responsibility of News Readers:

All of the above imposes an important responsibility on those who read and take in the news. This is the only place where responsibility of accurate judgment can truly lie. A good journalist or newspaperman will try to confirm what he reports, weeding out propaganda that might be posing as news, and honestly reporting the propaganda citizens should be aware of. Once he has done this, the journalist allows the reader to criticize and evaluate on his own terms. This is the privilege and responsibility of a citizen in a democracy.

CHAPTER 4
Are Modern News Outlets Legitimate Sources?

The presidential election in 2016 brought the question of the credibility of media into the spotlight in America. Fake news, bias in mainstream media, and other related topics have been debated hotly within the ensuing 12 months. And surveys done in recent times have proven that a lot of the largest news outlets in America aren't as trusted as they were before, with the right being particularly skeptical. Outlets such as ABC News and CNN have the largest audiences.

However, it turns out that the more trusted sources in the USA are British news outlets.

The Most and Least Trusted Outlets:

The Economist and the BBC are at the top of the list of the most trusted outlets by each ideological group in the USA, while Rush Limbaugh and BuzzFeed are the least trusted. News outlets that are more conservative appear to be least trusted within those groups that have more central or mixed political beliefs. Outlets that are more liberal-leaning, such as ThinkProgress and Mother Jones, are also ranking lower at this time than more major players such as The New York Times and The Wall Street Journal.

Where do Americans get their Information?

The outlets for news that are most trustworthy in the eyes of every group in America are not the most popular, though. U.S. citizens say that most of their news (politically) comes from Facebook, local TV channels, and networks such as Fox News and CNN. Fox News and CNN both had pretty high ratings of trust, as a whole, but within the ideological groups, there is still dispute about whether they really can be trusted. CNN and MSNBC are improving slightly, but Fox News is becoming less and less trusted.

Reliability of Claims by Major Networks:

When observed and fact-checked, most news networks tell lies on a consistent and regular basis. Fox News has had periods of times where only 10 percent of what they said was true. CNB and MSNBC has been caught lying over 44 percent of the time. CNN, on the other hand, had the best rating at 80 percent of their reports being either 50 percent true or better. However, you should be careful when it comes to using these numbers to make your conclusions.

Is CNN reliable as a News Source?

There was a time that CNN was a very reliable news source, but is this true these days, or not? The truth is that they are not always reliable. In addition, they might intentionally ignore important news items, resulting in a biased perception for their viewers.

CNN's Beginnings:

When CNN first began, they operated under Ted Turner, who wanted to report news instead of focusing on celebrities or other nonsense.

Many staff that joined CNN back then had a good feeling of joining a group who really wanted to report true news. This is how they gained their reputation of being an honest, reliable news source and some still see them as this.

The Merging of AOL and CNN:

Then there was the merger between AOL and CNN. AOL was acquiring the CNN network at the time and wanted to acquire new customers more than anything else. Some even believe that AOL wanted to lock customers in, make it so they couldn't leave, and get as much money out of them as possible. But CNN, at this time, had a culture of service and wanted to do good at that time. CNN workers expected there to be a gigantic clash when this merger hit and they were right. Managers began attempting to please their new AOL bosses, rather than trying to gather legitimate, unbiased news.

Fox News and CNN:

Around this same time period, Fox News was beginning to beat out CNN viewers in terms of ratings. How was this possible? Fox News was giving their audience the type of news they wanted to hear. However, the executives at Fox also knew that making the news about the celebrities and stars rather than the news content, finding polarizing and charismatic anchors and giving them free reign to say whatever they wanted, could work for making their ratings go up. Their idea was that this approach would seem far more exciting than CNN.

CNN Trying to Compete:

Eventually, CNN noticed what Fox was doing and tried out a similar strategy, and that's when Nancy Grace and Rick Sanchez were hired, along with Piers Morgan and more. Before this era, not many reports on CNN could do whatever they wanted and keep their job. Even the anchors who were capable and smart, such as Don Lemon, are not encouraged to give their opinions along with news, or even focus more on opinion than news. Many people who watch CNN these days will find that they are listening to the anchors telling what they think about a story, not what they know.

A Lack of Credibility:

News anchors are there to read the news, but this paradigm has changed. Now, news anchors say whatever they think will make them more interesting to viewers, often to the peril of their own credibility. Of course, this is also the fault of the line producers and executive producers who share responsibility in the de-evolution of news. But CNN does not work anymore because it has strayed too far from its roots. Ted Turner's way of doing things was the way to go, reporting on the stories rather than focusing on the celebrity of the anchors.

CNN's Declining Numbers:

In order for CNN to become a credible news source again, its anchors must remember that it's not about being the most exciting out there, but about being solid and reliable with their facts. Sometimes, this may involve reporting on "boring" news until something major happens, then they could cover a huge story as no other network can, reporting on facts, not opinion. The idea of being solid with reporting, but boring, may not be so appealing to the network, but the alternative isn't working for them.

The Necessity of Responsible Reporting:

When a news network stops reporting on the real news, and instead turns it into a popularity contest, no one will watch their air. In order to return to their previous integrity, an approach that is about the news, not the stars, is a must. This could help them re-earn their lost trust. When you are seeking out reliable news outlets, don't look for the most interesting characters or the most outlandish claims, instead seek out the facts. Let's look more into how to find the most credible online sources.

How to Determine Credible Online Sources:

Just about any person out there can make a webpage. Libraries, churches, government entities, businesses, and schools make websites to offer people the chance to learn more about them. Individual people can make blogs or personal websites to talk about their work, friends, families, or whatever else they desire. Corporations can also create websites to advertise their services and products, while political activities can promote their causes with websites. Any person who has online access and an idea can make one and put whatever they want on it.

More than 600 million websites (that are active) exist across the globe, and many of these are protected by anti-censorship and free speech laws. Owners of websites are able to print anything, whether it's true or false, with almost no consequences. With such a huge amount of content and so little censorship or fact-checking, teaching yourself how to determine which information is true and reliable can feel like quite a chore. However, not taking the time to do this could lead you to the wrong conclusions and some serious trouble. Fortunately, you can take some simple, easy steps to better evaluate a website's credibility and stay in the know.

How to Check Sources:

When you were finding this information, how was the source discovered by you? Top Google search results are usually won by the sites that have the largest budgets. Sources discovered through social media often encounter this same issue and bias. Look at the tips listed below to understand how you can find credible information online. This section is made for the average surfer of the Internet. For academic or professional research, there are other considerations, which we will cover in chapter seven of this book.

Begin with Recognized Sites:

If you had a choice between getting information about world news from The Wall Street Journal and Average Joe's Basement Rag, the majority of people would choose the Journal, since it's a known and trusted name to most. This also applies to research online. If you are hoping to find out how the election last week went, going to a trusted news outlet site is the perfect starting place. If you need investment tips, choose a company you believe in and then go to their webpage for the information you seek.

Better information might exist somewhere, but beginning with a business you know about already is the best way to get a smaller pool to begin with in your search. You can then choose to find more info from different pages or sources to compare to the first info you found. If you find information on Average Joe's Basement Rag that doesn't align with other information, on sources such as The Wall Street

Journal, odds are the information on the lesser-known source isn't very reliable.

Make sure it's Current:

Another tip you should pay attention to, especially when it comes to the Internet, is looking at an article's date, along with the dates on resources and studies mentioned in the article. If the article you're reading is mentioning a decade-old study, you might stop to wonder how reliable the information really is. This is the case, especially if studies have been done more recently on the same topic.

Check for Dead Links:

Another key indicator of a broken or outdated article is "dead" links. Many articles on websites have links inserted for credibility, but if these links are dead and don't lead anywhere, that article is likely very out of date. One link that no longer works is likely no cause for alarm, but multiple dead links is reason to be suspicious of the credibility of the source. One who creates a legitimate site will make sure their links are still working so those reading can find out more information, if needed.

Look for Credentials:

Another great way to find out whether online content or an article is legitimate is to look at the credentials of the author. When you are seeking data on a toothache, reading information from a professional dentist who has two decades of experience will yield you better results than reading a random blog by a hobbyist. If the website's author gives out a list of sources or references to prove her or his credentials, this is an even better sign.

Keep in mind that anyone can write what they want on the Internet, so just because a person claims they are a professional doesn't make them a real professional. A lot of websites, even those that are trusted, allow freelance writers or staff to write their articles, meaning that the writers might not be professionals. But good writers will at least use information gathered from professional or reliable sources.

Check the Domain and TLD:

One easy way to determine how credible a source online is, is to search for what the point or purpose of their page is, which can be seen by looking at the website address. Every site out there has a TLD (Top Level Domain) at the end of it. This is the part that comes after the period in the website name. For example, Google.com ends with .com, which allows you to see that the site is a commercial page. This is the most common ending online and any entity, business, or person can use it. Keep in mind that when you conduct your own research online, .com sites need more consideration and critical thinking than other sites.

Using Critical Thinking with Online Sources:

In order to get good information out of sources on the Internet, you need to learn about critical thinking. Critical thinking means evaluating sources like research findings, observable phenomena, facts, and data. Quality critical thinkers are able to discern reasonable opinions or conclusions from what they see, discriminating between worthless and useful data for making a choice. They are able to present logical, good reasons for their position.

Critical Thinking Examples:

- A nurse uses her skills of critical thinking to look at her patient's situation and decide what treatment to give them in the moment.

- A lawyer would look over evidence, using critical thinking to come up with a plan for winning a case.

- A plumber could use his critical thinking abilities to decide which tools he needs to fix an issue with someone's plumbing.

- Someone who needs a job could use critical thinking skills to decide whether they are qualified for an open job.

A List of Useful Skills in Critical Thinking:

1. **Clarification**: Clarification means being able to state information in another way that is simpler to understand.

2. **Analysis**: Analysis means being able to examine information, understanding what it both represents and means in practice and theory.

3. **Evaluation**: Evaluation means being able to judge and assess how valid an idea is.

4. **Inference**: Inference is knowing how to come up with conclusions using the data you've been given.

5. **Explanation:** This is related to clarification and relies on being able to state information clearly, adding your own idea to the data.

6. **Judgment:** Similar to evaluation, this involves assessing a piece of data or a concept you've been presented with.

7. **Interpretation:** Interpretation means understanding the information you've been introduced to, communicating its meaning in a simple way.

8. **Objectivity:** Objectivity means that you can be fair in your evaluations of information, holding back your own biases.

9. **Solving Problems:** Solving problems is another crucial ability that means

coming up with a solution and then applying it.

10. **Reasoning:** Reasoning means being able to think in a logical way about a problem or question.

Demonstrating the Skills of Critical Thinking:

Critical thinking is an important skill to have, in many situations, such as seeking a job. It can be used on your applications, interviews, and in cover letters. In order to get better at critical thinking, imagine roles you've held in the past, and think about when you've needed to evaluate the information you had to fix an issue. This is critical thinking at work. This can also be applied to all news and information you are exposed to. Try to use the skills listed above, every time you encounter a piece of information, even from a credible source.

73

Using Critical Thinking to Dig Deeper:

If you're evaluating information and still are not certain, take this time to dig deeper into the subject. Look for other pieces of writing on the website, written by the same person if possible. Is their opinion sound on other subjects? Is their writing strong and consistent? Do their articles seem like they were made up or unbelievable? Social media sites, especially Facebook, are notorious for sharing fake news articles. If you check out other articles on the website, you will be better able to determine whether the website has a bias (which almost every site does). This will help you better evaluate what the site is telling you.

Grammar Errors and Typos:

Grammar errors and typos are another way to determine whether the website is a credible source or not. A person who makes a legitimate site is determined to give their viewers real, factual information. This means taking care of the grammar and spelling to make the website professional and reliable.

Go to the Library:

Most people get their information online, and it's a great source, but when it comes to accuracy, it's hard to beat the library. The majority of libraries out there will allow their customers to use their online research tools, so you are able to do research from home. Libraries are hooked up to databases full of research, a lot of which call for a subscriptions and cannot be found using typical search engines.

Using these databases, you can search for written information in online books, journals, and even in print. Most of the resources here have been peer reviewed, meaning that it's usually professional information that has been approved and reviewed by other credible sources in the same field.

Always Look beyond the first Information Source:

Lastly, regardless of where you find your information, you should always check it again using other reliable sources. This can be done by checking sources at the library or just be doing extra research online. If you see the same data come up on multiple legitimate sites and in written publications, it's safe to believe that the information is correct.

CHAPTER 5
Who Owns these Media Platforms?

The U.S. landscape of the media is dominated by massive corporations. Throughout a history of acquisitions and mergers, these businesses have managed to concentrate their power over all that we read, hear, and see. A lot of times, these businesses control every step from first production stages to the very final distribution. So, who specifically owns what in terms of the media?

Radio and Television:

Broadcasters earn billions of dollars in profits, using the airwaves of public sources at no cost to them. As a way to give back, these broadcasters are instructed to give programming that fulfills needs of the community. But instead, lobbyists have found ways to make broadcast companies have an even easier time using up free airspace, neglecting to do anything worthwhile for the public. Let's look at the broadcasters that own radio and television:

- **CBS Corporation:** CBS Corporation owns operations in nearly every single media and entertainment field, including cable TV, broadcast TV, local TV, licensing and merchandising, music, advertising, publishing, and much, much more.

- **Comcast Corporation:** This company took over most of NBC Universal in 2011, which was approved by the Federal

Communications Commission. This gigantic merger combined one of the globe's largest motion picture and TV show producer with the country's biggest cable company and service Internet provider. The media holdings of Comcast reach nearly every single home in the United States, now. The company serves customers in almost 40 states. In addition, Comcast just entered into a Verizon partnership which allows each business to sell and market the other's products and services.

- **News Corp:** This company has media holdings in FOX, Broadcasting, Fox Business Channel, FX, National Geographic, and print publications like The New York post, the Wall Street Journal, TV Guide, and more. They also own film production business such as

Fox Searchlight Pictures, 20th Century Fox, and more.

Telecommunications and Cable:

Having access to the Internet (especially high speed broadband) is essentially now a necessity for the public, like electricity or water. But despite how important the Internet is, access to broadband in America is not universal, and far from it. A lot of U.S. citizens are still let behind in terms of the modern digital divide, held back from accessing the social, economic, and political resources online.

Meanwhile, phone and cable companies, which are controlling the Internet, refuse to offer broadband to the places that are in direst need of it and even try to block out communities from creating solutions to the problem. Let's take a look at some of these companies now.

- **AT&T:** AT&T is a gigantic provider of wireless services in the USA and is the biggest business offering local telephone services in the country. The company offers its business to more than 97 percent of the population and also offers cable TV.

- **Comcast Corporation:** Mentioned earlier, Comcast Corporation owns media holdings in nearly every single American household. It's soon to merge with Verizon, where its power will become even more concentrated than it is now.

- **Verizon:** This company is the biggest provider of wireless services in America, serving more than 98 percent of the population in America. It just recently partnered up with Time Warner Cable, Comcast, and Cox Communications. These companies will all now sell and market the other's products and services.

Print:

The media consolidation mentioned above has created some hard times for the industry of print, which now seems outdated. Back in the 1990s, when this industry was doing very well, companies of big media used up to 27 percent of profit margins to purchase new properties, instead of investing money into their existing products, making the quality better or planning out the future. Now, people are pushing the possibility of companies to own both a broadcasting station and a newspaper in the same exact market.

- **News Corp:** This company has media holdings, including National

Geographic, FX, Fox Business Channel, Fox, and Fox Broadcasting Company. They also own the TV Guide channel, the New York Post, and the Wall Street Journal, as mentioned earlier. They also own Shine Limited, ESPN Star Sports, STAR Taiwan, STAR India, Baby TV, Elite Sports Limited, the Film Zone, City Vibe, City Stars, City Family, City Mix, Movie City, LAPTV, and NGC Network Latin America.

- They also own NGC Network International, STAR Movies, STAR World, the Voyage Channel, FOX History and Entertainment, NEXT, Fox Crime, Fox International Channels, Nat Geo Wild, Nat Geo Music, Nat Geo Adventure, National Geographic U.S, Big Ten Network, and much, much more.

- **The Washington Post:** This company is involved with online and print publishing of magazines and newspapers, cable TV systems and television broadcasting. They own Kaplan, Inc., also, which offers services of higher education, professional training, language instruction, and test preparation.

The Internet:

Gigantic companies such as Google, Facebook, and Apple are slowly changing the landscape of the Internet. As the businesses attempt to force us into their closed-off versions of the world wide web (and to marketing companies who stand to benefit from using our personal data), it becomes ever-more important to protect personal rights of those who use the Internet.

- **Microsoft:** Microsoft is the producer of Windows, which is the most commonly utilized operating system for computers on the globe. The company also owns multiple online services and software, including Bing.com, the second ranked search engine.

- **Apple:** Apple has created the computer system called Macintosh and many different consumer products such as the iPod, iPhone, and iPad. The company runs iTunes, the biggest music store in the world and distributes its services and products all over the nation.

- **Google:** Google is the world's biggest online advertising seller and the most popular search engine available. It sells many different services online and also created the operating system, Android.

The Corporate Concentration of Power:

In the year 1983, about 50 different corporations were in control of most of the news media outlets in America. These days, news media ownership is now concentrated into the control of only six extremely powerful corporations. These businesses control the majority of what we read, hear, and watch every day. They are in control of television networks, music labels, publishing houses, magazines, newspapers, movie studios, some websites, and cable channels. Unfortunately, the average American citizen does not stop to wonder where their entertainment and news is coming from.

Addicted to Entertainment:

Most American citizens do not bother themselves about who is in control of the media they are constantly taking in. However, they should care. Whether we realize it or not, all of us are strongly affected and influenced by the stories and messages being forced on us by the media. The average citizen in the United States watches over 150 hours of TV each and every month. Actually, most citizens of America will feel uncomfortable in a physical sense if they cannot watch or listen to something for too long. Unfortunately, most of us are so addicted to entertainment and news and most of what we consume is being controlled by smaller and smaller pools of corporate power every year.

The Six Media Giants:

The six companies mentioned that control the media in the United States today are NBC Universal, CBS Corporation, Rupert Murdoch's news Corp., Viacom, Walt Disney, and Time Warner. In combination, these six power structures dominate the entertainment and news fields in America. And even the media areas that the six corporations don't own yet are getting more and more concentrated as time goes on. For instance, Clear channel owns more than 1000 radio broadcasting sources across the country, while companies such a Microsoft, Yahoo, and Google are dominating the Internet more and more.

However, these big six companies should be our main concern. When the companies can control everything being watched, read, and heard by Americans, they can also control a lot of what they are thinking. It's not a coincidence that they are called television "programs." In the year '83, 50 corporations controlling all of the media in the United States was bad enough, but ever since, control over media outlets is becoming more concentrated. In our modern day, six media giants are dominating the rest of the sphere. To get a more realistic picture of how far this actually goes, let's look at what the media outlets own.

<u>Time Warner:</u>

- Time Inc.
- HBO (Home Box Office)
- Turner Broadcasting System, Inc.
- CW Network
- Warner Bros. Entertainment
- New Line Cinema
- TMZ
- Cinemax
- TBS
- Cartoon Network
- America Online
- TNT
- Movefone
- MapQuest
- Castle Rock
- Fortune

- Sports Illustrated
- Marie Claire
- People Magazine
- Fortune

<u>Viacom:</u>

- Paramount Home Entertainment
- Paramount Pictures
- Comedy Central
- BET (Black Entertainment Television)
- CMT (Country Music Television)
- MTV
- MTV Canada
- Logo
- Nick at Nite
- Nick Jr.
- Nickelodeon
- Nick Magazine
- Noggin
- Spike TV

- VH1
- TV Land
- The Movie Channel
-

Walt Disney

- Disney Publishing
- ABC Television Network
- Disney Channel
- ESPN Inc.
- A&E
- SOAPnet
- Lifetime
- Buena Vista Theatrical Productions
- Buena Vista Records
- Buena Vista Home Entertainment
- Hollywood Records
- Disney Records
- Touchstone Pictures
- Miramax Films
- Walt Disney Pictures

- Buena Vista Games
- Pixar Animation Studios
- Hyperion Books

News Corporation

- Fox Television Stations
- Dow Jones & Company, Inc.
- Fox Searchlight Pictures
- The New York Post
- Beliefnet
- Fox Kids Europe
- Fox Business Network
- Fox Sports Net
- Fox News Channel
- FX
- Fox Television Networl
- MySpace
- My Network TV
- Phoenix InfoNews Channel
- News Limited News

- Phoenix Movies Channel
- Sky PerfecTV
- STAR TV India
- Speed Channel
- STAR TV Taiwan
- STAR World
- Times Literary Supplement Magazine
- Times Higher Education Supplement Magazine
- 20th Century Fox Home Entertainment
- Times of London
- 20th Century Fox International
- Sky Radio Netherlands
- 20th Century Fox Television
- DIRECTV
- Zondervan
- 20th Century Fox Studios
- Sky Radio Germany
- The Wall Street Journal
- Fox Interactive Media
- Fox Broadcasting Company

- FOXTEL
- ReganBooks
- Sky Italia
- The National Geographic Channel
- HarperCollins Publishers
- National Rugby League
- News Outdoor
- Sky Radio Denmark
- News Interactive
- Radio Veronica
- STAR
-

<u>NBC Universal</u>

- Bravo
- NBC Sports
- Universal Studio Home Video
- Telemundo
- CNBC
- Oxygen
- Trio

- SciFi Magazine
- Paxson Communications
- Universal Parks & Resorts
- NBC news
- NBC Television Network
- MSNBC
- Universal Pictures
- Syfy (Sci Fi Channel)
- USA Network
- NBC Universal Television Distribution
- Focus Features
- Weather Channel
- NBC Universal Television Studio
-

CBS Corporation

- Showtime
- CBS News
- CW Network
- Westwood One Radio Network
- CBS Radio Inc.

- CBS Television Network

- CBS Sports

- CNET

- Infinity Broadcasting

- CBS Consumer Products

- Simon & Schuster

- CBS Outdoor

- TV.com

-

The media corporations listed above are not in existence to share truthful information with the U.S public. Instead, they exist for the sole purpose of making profits and these corporations won't do anything that could possibly harm the relationships they have going with mega advertisers (like pharmaceutical businesses). No matter what, these huge corporations that own the media will find ways to support the ideological beliefs and points of view of those who own and sponsor them.

Trust in Media is at an All-time Low:

Thankfully, a higher and higher number of U.S citizens are beginning to realize that they shouldn't have trust in the mainstream media. A new poll done by Gallup showed that 57 percent of Americans have either no trust in the media, or very little trust, which is a record. This is one of the many reasons why alternative media has gone through a lot of growth in recent times. Mainstream media sources are losing their credibility increasingly, leading Americans to look in other places for real information about the world.

Do you believe that any mainstream media news sources would be honest about the fact that the Federal Reserve is harming our country, or that we are going through a bubble of derivatives that may destroy the whole financial system of the globe? Would you expect to hear, from anyone in the mainstream media, about Goldman Sachs's harmful greed or the fact that America is becoming deindustrialized?

The Need for Independence in Finding the Truth:

It's true that there are some courageous journalists that slip through the cracks and share the truth every once in a while, but over all, certain topics are off limit in this sphere. And as American citizens become hungrier for real news and increasingly fed up with what is shown on mainstream outlets these days, learning how to discern the truth is more important than ever.

The Harmful Impact of Media Consolidation:

These days, corporations own basically all of our media news outlets. Concerned only with the bottom line, these corporate interest groups are gutting newsrooms and cutting out journalists all over the country. In addition, a lot of these corporate power structures are finding ways to dodge the ownership rules of the FCC and finding ways to monopolize more and more markets across America.

The higher number of independent news outlets a nation has, the more diversity of information it will have access to, and the reverse of this is equally true. The FCC closing down loopholes in ownership laws would help this, along with creating policies that could diversity ownership in media.

Consolidation has been running wild in the broadband and cable industries, where businesses such as Comcast spend unthinkable amounts of money to get rid of competition, instead of building out their services to communities that need them or even improving their existing products and services for current customers. Meanwhile, internet access at home continues to soar, leaving people behind, especially those with lower incomes.

More Effects of Media Consolidation:

Media undoubtedly plays a huge role in our modern world. It's nearly impossible to avoid media within an average day out in a city or even at home. Six gigantic corporations are aware of this and are now attempting to completely control the world of media. But is this a good direction to be heading in? Is this big corporate takeover more harmful than good? There is no shortage of debate on the media consolidation topic.

A lot of customers think that it's a convenient turn of events since a single business can control various services, allowing customers to have their TV service, internet service, and phone service on a single bill.

But although this is convenient and helpful for some, it does limit our choices in these services, as customers. Only a select few businesses can afford to offer related products and services, meaning that they and they alone have the power to lower quality and raise prices on the services they offer. This possibility is very likely since customers won't have access to these services without the corporations under their terms. The corporations then have complete power over us.

Less Power to Choose for the Customer:

In the scenario described above, which is happening increasingly as we speak, the consumer no longer has the power to choose and are forced to agree with the low quality and high prices of media services. Therefore, convenience is not more important than quality and stopping media consolidation is the only method for retaining its quality once again.

This chapter has gone over the specific six corporations controlling our media outlets, including CBS, Time Warner, Viacom, Disney, News Corp, and GE. These corporations are in sole control over what we, as American citizens, have access to seeing. We already stated the fact that back in 1983, almost all of the media was already controlled by 50 different businesses. Now, 90 percent of it is under the control of just six corporate super powers. This is a serious issue because it puts an inherent limit on what we have access to seeing and reading.

Some people are all for this because they believe it offers better diversity and quality of content, but it actually does the opposite of that. The majority of the time, these companies are owned by a select few powerful people who have always been in power, while smaller businesses are owned by under-represented people. Our media would have a more diverse voice if the owners were more diverse and didn't just represent corporate interests and money. When money is the sole driver of content, it is going to be very shallow indeed.

Watching Less TV:

The corporate takeover of media may be inevitable, in a sense, but people can start by making sure they watch less TV, in addition to applying critical thinking skills to that which they do read, listen to, or watch. Pay attention to where your news and information is coming from and what the goal is behind what you're absorbing. Although we may not be able to control media consolidation, we can control how much of it we choose to partake in and believe. Do not support the companies that are taking away your choice.

CHAPTER 6
What is Fake News and How can you Spot it?

The concept "fake news" was first catapulted into mainstream discussion when Donald Trump had his very first press conference as the official President elect. He refused to listen to Jim Acosta of CNN, while he shouted "You are fake news!" Ever since this, our President has been accusing major news outlets of being "fake news" on Twitter, especially the New York Times and CNN. But where did this term come from and why is it being used and repeated so often lately?

<u>The Origin of Fake News:</u>

The phenomenon of stretching the truth for the gain of political viewpoints is not new. This is basic propaganda, which, as we explained in the first few chapters, has been a part of human societies for many decades (or even more). Octavian even used misinformation to beat out Marc Antony back during the times of the Romans. After this, he even created a youthful, flattering image of himself and changed his name. Fake news and propaganda also has plenty of history in the politics of America.

Propaganda in the 20th Century:

As mass communication skyrocketed, propaganda also grew in persuasive power and scale when ideologies struggled against each other in the 20th century. In the first world war, the government of Britain was very effective in their use of propaganda to get their population set against the Germans. Germany, at that time, was called "The Hun." The German Nazi party also used the increasing mass media to create a base of power and then consolidated that power in the country during the '30s, encouraging discrimination through racial stereotyping.

In the world war that resulted, the machine of propaganda was used by every side in the media spectrum and even appeared in cartoons and related entertainment forms. For instance, Donald Duck was depicted in a Nazi world as an attempt to sell off war bonds in the U.S. This style of propaganda was mostly controlled and funded by the governments. However, the obvious bias it had within it faltered as the struggles between ideologies became less obvious. In addition, populations grew used to the newer forms of mass communication and thus could see through these tactics more easily.

Fake News and the Internet:

The increasingly popularity of the "fake news" topic during the year 2016 wasn't the same as the state-controlled methods of propaganda used in the 20th century. What happened here, oftentimes, were smaller groups of individuals using interaction on social media, combined with algorithms, to make exaggerated, hyperbolic news articles about the presidential election. Internet fake news and propaganda are similar, however, in many ways. These are both ways of muddling the truth in favor of emotional persuasion and attempting to create action in listeners and readers.

Though these actions appear political on the surface, the 2016 US election motivation wasn't necessarily political. A lot of the creators of this content were just trying to earn a quick buck by gaining audiences and creating content that could generate ad revenue online. Before the world wide web, gaining audience members and publishing fake news stories that were profitable were not possible for a few different reasons:

- **Cost and Distribution:** Before the internet, distributing information on such a large scale was extremely expensive and therefore inaccessible for the average person.

- **Regulation and Law:** Since it was so costly to share information in this way, far fewer people had access to doing this. The ones that were a part of it had to follow media laws and were regulated according to standards. Fake news being published would have probably ended up with someone getting sued.

- **Trust and Audiences:** Creating a big audience required a lot of time back then, and since it cost money to build on and acquire trust from audience members, creating fake news stories would have damaged the company's reputation, resulting in loss of readers and funding.

But around the year 2007, this information exchange gate was opened up as social media became more prevalent. Twitter and Facebook allowed users to trade data and information on a larger scare, which was impossible before. They also were able to use publishing platforms, creating dynamic webpages easily. Essentially, the barriers listed above to making fake news possible were abolished. Let's look at how they changed.

- **Cost and Distribution:** The expenses of distributing (as in sharing on social networks) and publishing (on sites such as WordPress), became essentially free.

- **Regulation and Law:** With these cheaper expenses, a lot more operators became involved in trading data and information on the Internet. The flow of law-regulated information became impossible to control as it became a gigantic tidal wave.

- **Trust and Audiences:** Since the costs were so much lower, and often free, reputations were not as important to uphold.

The 2016 Campaign and Fake News:

Once the barriers of finances were removed, fake news was more prevalent within 2016 than the previous years. The election campaign at that time made an almost perfect backdrop for this. The presidential campaign became a matter of global discussion and the debate became increasingly polarized in many different ways. Donald Trump was the essential ingredient in this, with a campaign that claimed the anti-establishment stance and his words against Hillary Clinton.

In addition, Trump hinted at popular conspiracy theories, suggesting that Cruz's father had something to do with JFK's assassination and briefly mentioning Obama being born outside of the USA. He also called climate change a hoax repeatedly. His wildcard tactics certainly got the attention it aimed to get, fueled by controversial suggestions about banning Muslims from the U.S and building a wall between the U.S and Mexico.

The candidate's unpredictable statements and his open distrust in his political opponents led to the creation of false news in support of Trump. When you are in a political sphere that is so unpredictable, you are more susceptible to truth distortion and ridiculous hyperbole.

Viral, Fake Headlines:

Headlines about Hillary selling military weapons to ISIS, the Pope supporting Trump, and numerous stories about Hillary's emails; each of these fake news headlines were viral immediately after being put on Facebook. They were so shared and popular that the website BuzzFeed created an analysis about the way these articles were more popular than true Facebook news. But other people think that social media's filter bubble is to blame, which involves showing Facebook users only content that they agree with or like and hiding anything they wouldn't. Some believe that this approach causes distortion to the playing field.

Theoretically, someone could set up a website, buy their audience from a page on Facebook, then spread false news stories on that page. With a headline that is strong and outlandish enough, this story could instantly turn into viral material, bringing in a lot of money for the one who published it. Facebook could, if it discovered the news was fake, degrade that page's domain. However, since the entry barriers are so low, the publisher could instantly create another webpage, repeating his previously successful method.

Does Fake News Influence Readers?

Once election day passed, the spreaders of fake news were called out by many different outlets of news media. Some announced that Facebook was to blame for Trump winning, due to the fake news being allowed through onto newsfeeds. Although the statistics of over 60 percent of American citizens going to social networks to get their news, and over 40 percent only using Facebook for news, can be called upon to prove that fake news does influence readers, these statistics are very general. It's impossible to know what the fake news numbers actually mean in terms of how much the news influences. For example, how could you quantify a Like on Facebook with this?

Less Influence than it Seems?

Consider also that a huge number of Facebook audiences on pages dedicated to fake news are actually not real or even from the USA. This proves that fake news doesn't have as much influence as some may fear. To support this claim, a study done by Stanford said that in order for this fake news to have had a huge impact on the presidential election results, one fake news article would have had the same impact as nearly 40 different presidential campaign advertisements. The concept of fake news is probably more annoying than something that has a devastating impact. But the word has turned into something that mainstream media is now being accused of.

Co-Opting the Concept:

Many believe that the idea of fake news has been taken on my commentators and politicians and applied to any story that doesn't support their cause or that they don't agree with. This makes the concept basically meaningless. Ever since the presidential election in 2016, fears have taken hold that fake news will become more popular in Europe to change the results of Germany and France's elections. In these countries, groups on the far right are hoping to get ahead, such as the Alternative fur Deutschland and the Front national. Google and Facebook have claimed that they will be stricter about false information, but this remains to be seen.

How to tell Fake News from Real News:

How can you tell whether a source of news is reliable or not? How can you tell whether a story in the news is true or just fake news? We mentioned active links as a way to tell, but these are not always very reliable when it comes to news stories. There isn't one single automatic method for telling how reliable a news story is.

The Well-known News Sources:

At times, it's hard to even trust a newspaper that most believe is reputable. However, with a few exceptions, you can count on the more reliable online news sources being the tried and true organizations that are best-known. They are still the ones who offer the original material online. If you come across some information on a webpage and need to find out whether or not it's true, you can just check whether it's on a source of reputable stories. These would be the main news agencies and main newspaper companies. This is the foundational criterion for fact-checking in journalism; check out your information across multiple sources online or in a library.

What about Credibility?

The next question is how to truly evaluate a source's credibility. You could practice by reading multiple texts that talk about the use of language in the production of news, news' impact on local situations, professionalization, the impact news has on social situations, and political economies of news companies. When you focus on the type of language used in the news stories, you can cut through the prejudices and biases you might have without realizing it. A fair depiction of the story and a news source's credibility has a lot to do with whether or not the "us vs. them" dynamic is created.

Depending on which perspective you are looking at the circumstances from, these shift. If you notice that a story you are reading attempts to explain the situation from more than one perspective, that's a good sign. A good news story should offer you questions to answer, not a solid opinion or feeling of closure after encountering it. Pay attention to what imagery and words the story calls to mind, which should be one of fairness. No matter what, being critical of news from the mainstream media is a good idea, no matter how credible the organization presenting the information is. If you follow these guidelines, you will find it much easier to discern the truth from mainstream information.

CHAPTER 7
Tips for Evaluating Information Online

Our country is suffering from a shortage of critical thinking. This is partially due to the overabundance of bad information on the internet and partially due to the short attention spans of the average American. Let's look over the reasons for this, so we can start working towards fixing it.

A Shortage of Critical Thinking:

Children these days are having a hard time taking the information they learn and applying it to their real world experience. This is a serious issue, not only a philosophical one. As a society, we need to do better and return to the use of critical thinking. As technology takes over, a serious dilemma is appearing. People are finding traditional methods of thinking and finding out the truth from media less important to their real life situations.

Instead, most would rather play a game, learn how to download movies faster, or learn some coding techniques. But adults are also facing similar challenges. A lot of us feel not only left behind in terms of technology, but out of the loop because of fake news. How are we to tell what's real and what isn't? How are we to stay informed? Instead of making the right choices, we are instead pressured to be as productive as possible. Senior citizens are demoralized for their difficulties in keeping up with the world of news on social media, instead of revered for their experience and wisdom.

The Harm of Instant Gratification:

The climate of fake news has fostered a habit of seeking instant gratification and answers, instead of thoughtful questions or better quality consideration. However, quicker answers just means refusing to delve deeper into real world problems and preferring substance-less, fake news over real world questions and answers. Everyone already has the answers they seek on their smart phones, but do we know how to analyze these answers and get the truth from them?

The Habit of Instant Answers:

The modern American public has taught itself that finding the answers as quickly as possible is the sign of education and intelligence, not being able to think critically or determine the truth from the information we are given. But real intelligence isn't about how quickly one can pull up an answer. Actually, the more time we put into our smart phones, the lazier we get with our minds.

Getting Excited about Learning:

Rather than relying on what we are fed from these increasingly less trustworthy news sources, why not return to getting excited about learning and thinking? What about learning how to wonder again? We must know how to take the information we are given and turn it into something relevant by stepping away from the smart phones and applying some good old-fashioned critical thinking. A nation can only be as strong as its weakest link, meaning that something needs to change as soon as possible. What does evaluating online sources have to do with the ability of critical thinking? Let's take a look now.

Critical Thinking and Evaluating Online Sources:

In this chapter, the questions given to you will aid you in evaluating websites and information, in general, to use both academically and to form your own opinion of the news. Make sure that you look at what is involved in a few different categories before you make a choice about the source's quality. With critical thinking skills, you will not be fooled by negative propaganda or false online sources. Follow these rules to make sure you are always using your brain to the best of your ability.

Tips for Effectively Evaluating Online Info:

Since most people find their news and information online, it's important to know how to evaluate the information you find there. Let's look over some important considerations you must make to ensure that the source you're reading is legitimate. Ask yourself the following questions.

How'd you Discover this Source?

The way you found this source will help you begin on the evaluation of how valid the site is and whether it's trustworthy. Let's look at some questions you can ask yourself to get a better idea.

- Was the source found using Google? The quality or accuracy of information found online can vary a lot, unlike databases in academic libraries. Make sure you are searching carefully!

- Who recommended this source to you? Was it someone reliable? This can help you determine whether or not what you're reading is legitimate.

- Was the source cited by a credible source, such as a scholarly article or research paper? Does it have a reputable site linked on it?

What's the Domain of the Site?

This step can be thought of as decoding the Internet address, also known as the website's URL. How the site originated can tell you a lot about the website's purpose or mission. Here are some common domains and what they mean:

- **.com:** This is a commercial or business website.

- **.org:** This usually signifies a non-profit or advocacy site.

- **.net:** A network organization website or service provider.

- **.gov:** This signifies an official, federal government website.

- **.edu:** A site with this at the end signifies a University, typically.

- **.uk:** This is a website from the United Kingdom.

Who created this Website?

Many pages have an "About" section where you can learn about the creator of the site. IF the site you're on doesn't, that's a red flag. Try to find relevant data about the website's author. Anyone on the web can act like they are an expert on a subject. Here are some questions to ask yourself:

- Do you see the author's name somewhere on the page? Are they affiliated with the institution or organization?

- Are the author's credentials listed and are they relevant in terms of the information on the website?

- Is there contact information, such as a phone number and mailing address provided for the website?

Is the Information Objective and Accurate?

The Internet does not have any controls or standards for information accuracy, meaning it can be used by just about anyone to voice their opinions and thoughts.

- Is the information being presented accurate and based on factual data or statistics? Do you see a bibliography anywhere?

- Can you compare the website information to relevant sources and find consistent information?

- Is there a specific bias or point of view being pushed by the website? Is someone going to profit from you believing what it says?

- Is there advertising present on the page? This could have an effect on the accuracy of what you're reading.

Is the Website Current or Old?

This question can help you realize both how current the information is and whether the website is maintained or not, as mentioned in chapter four.

- When did this page get created?

- Is the news information current on this site?

- Are the website's links functional and current?

- Are there dates showing when the page was last updated?

Is the Page Functioning Well?

How easy a site is to use, along with its ability to give you the data you need, prove whether or not it's actually functional.

- Is there an index or site map included on the page?

- Can you search on the website?

- Can you easily navigate the website?

The tips listed above are especially important when it comes to deciphering information for academic reasons, but following these guidelines will help you with finding the truth, in general, when it comes to online information.

CONCLUSION

Thank you for reading *Debating Fake News: A Guide with Critical Thinking Strategies on How to Extract the Truth from Fake News and Alternative Facts in the Media.* Hopefully you now have a better understanding both of the concept of "fake news" and the results it can have in society.

Critical thinking is more important now than ever. As the news becomes increasingly biased and we all struggle to escape from being bombarded with articles full of immature slander, knowing how to sift through the fluff is a must. A democracy depends on the ability of its citizens to determine what's true and to form their own opinions. This responsibility starts with you! Learn how to decipher propaganda from the truth by asking yourself who created the message, what they stand to benefit from spreading it, and whether or not it serves you.

If you're new to critical thinking and viewing news sources with skepticism, please note that it will require practice until you get good at it. Then, you will be able to decipher the truth from the sources you see.

Thanks again for reading and if you enjoyed this book, please take the time to leave it a positive review on Amazon! Good luck.

www.ingramcontent.com/pod-product-compliance
Lightning Source LLC
Chambersburg PA
CBHW070809240726
48654CB00007B/278